SNOWBOARDING BLAST

SNOWBOARD SLOPESTYLE

by Karen Grimaldos

CAPSTONE PRESS
a capstone imprint

Published by Capstone Press, an imprint of Capstone
1710 Roe Crest Drive, North Mankato, Minnesota 56003
capstonepub.com

Library of Congress Cataloging-in-Publication Data is available on the Library of Congress website.
ISBN: 9798875255960 (hardcover)
ISBN: 9798875255915 (paperback)
ISBN: 9798875255922 (ebook PDF)

Summary: In snowboard slopestyle, riders face obstacles and fly off huge jumps. They pull off amazing midair tricks that impress crowds and judges. Readers will learn about how snowboard slopestyle courses are set up, how the events are scored, and which stars are leading the way in these exciting competitions.

Editorial Credits
Editor: Carrie Sheely; Designer: Hilary Wacholz; Media Researcher: Rebekah Hubstenberger; Production Specialist: Tori Abraham

Image Credits
Alamy: Action Plus Sports Images/Pierre Teyssot, 11; Getty Images: Al Bello, 6, 19, Alexis Boichard/Agence Zoom, 24-25, Cameron Spencer, 4-5, 18, 22, Clive Mason, 16-17, David Ramos, 8-9, 12, 15, 20, 23, Doug Pensinger, 14, iStock/technotr, cover, Maddie Meyer, 13, Patrick Smith, 27, Sam Mellish/In Pictures, 21, Tom Pennington, 10; Newscom: Kyodo, 29, Wolfgang Kofler/ZUMAPRESS, 26

Design Elements
Shutterstock: AlexanderTrou, kostins, Rosovskyi SAI A.D.A, sergio34

Printed and bound in China. 006459

TABLE OF CONTENTS

Words in **bold** are in the glossary.

CHAPTER 1

AN INCREDIBLE RUN

A snowboarder takes off down a steep hill. She speeds toward a rail. Seconds before reaching it, she jumps up. Now she's sliding on the rail! She jumps off backward and zips toward another rail.

BEIJING 2022

Now it's time for midair tricks. On her first jump, she grabs the board. On the next jump, she spins. The third jump is the highest. She flips and lands perfectly. What an amazing **run**! Will she earn the gold medal?

LET'S TALK SNOWBOARD SLOPESTYLE!

down-flat-down: a feature that starts sloping downward, flattens out, and then slopes downward again

feature: a natural or man-made obstacle used to perform a trick

grab: to hold on to the edge of a snowboard during a trick

jib: a non-snow surface that is used to perform tricks; it also means riding on an object

kinked rail: a feature that is not completely flat

rail: a thin feature snowboarders perform tricks on

rainbow rail: a curved rail shaped like a rainbow

rotation: a spin of the body

run: a ride down the slopestyle course

CHAPTER 2

THE SLOPESTYLE DIFFERENCE

What makes slopestyle different from other snowboarding events? **Obstacles**! These are often called features. Snowboarders jump, ride, or slide on features called jibs. Jibs include ramps, rails, **ledges**, and **boxes**. Slopestyle courses start with a jib section.

OAKLEY
UNION
UNION

The courses end with three big jumps. Riders fly high into the air. They spin. They flip. They grab their boards. Riders show off hard tricks to **impress** judges. Why? They all want the top score!

Riders need to be ready for anything! Each course is different. Rails might have sections that slope up or down. They can be made of different materials. Snow and weather conditions can make riding hard!

WHAT'S ON THE COURSE?

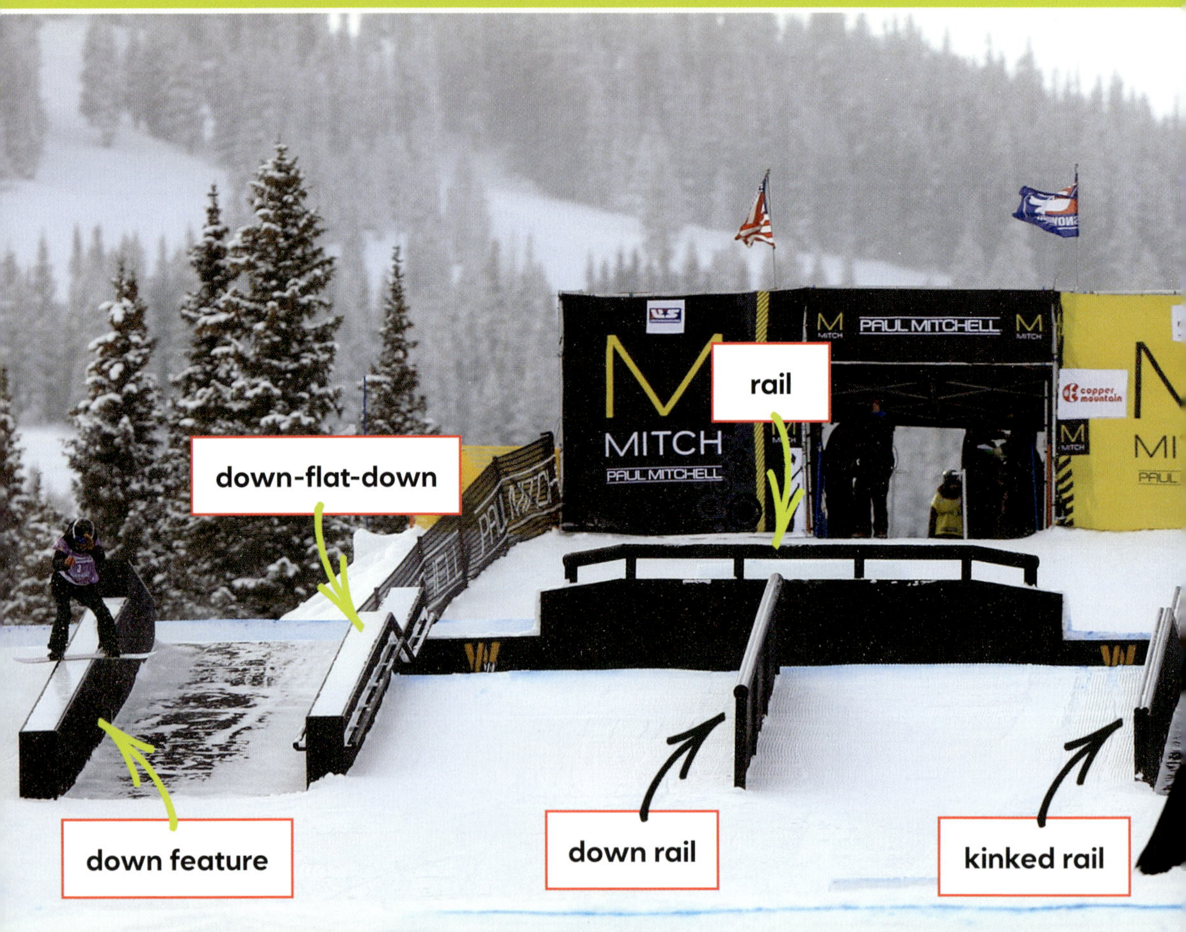

SLOPESTYLE SNOWBOARD FEATURES

Slopestyle riders have boards that help them perform at their best. These boards help them balance and do tricks.

CHAPTER 3

COMPETITIONS AND SCORING

It's competition time! Each rider does a run alone. The riders compete in rounds. Only riders with the top scores can move on to the next round. The finals are the last round. This is when the riders try to land their best tricks.

Tricks make up 60 percent of a rider's score. Tricks with more spins get higher points. The highest score a rider can get is 100 points.

What else does it take to get on the winners' **podium**? Judges look at how high riders go and their landings. They want riders to show their own **style**. Judges also look at how hard the tricks are and how well they are done.

Many top riders train year-round. They work out to build strength. Snowboarders need strong lower body muscles. Riders can use trampolines and foam pits to practice midair tricks. Trainers help riders perform at their best.

FACT

Slopestyle snowboarders sometimes practice on homemade courses. They use water jugs, skateboards, and even picnic tables as jibs!

Chris Corning competing at the 2022 Olympics

Top competitions include the X Games, the Winter Olympics, and the World Championships. The World Cup has several events in a **season**. The top scorer at the end of the season is the overall winner.

Novalie Engholm competing at the 2025 World Championships

FACT

Slopestyle snowboarding became an Olympic sport in the 2014 Winter Olympics.

CHAPTER 4

SLOPESTYLE STARS

In 2023, British rider Mia Brookes made history. How? By winning gold in slopestyle at the World Championships. She was 16. That made her the youngest snowboard world champion ever!

Mia Brookes at the 2023 World Championships

Cameron Spalding competing in a World Cup event

Canadian Cameron Spalding has been snowboarding since he was 3 years old. He was the overall winner in the 2024-2025 World Cup season.

Mark McMorris was the first snowboarder to win an Olympic medal three times in a row. The Canadian rider won bronze in the 2014, 2018, and 2022 Olympics.

Mark McMorris with his bronze Olympic medal in 2022

Snowboarders are known for pushing the limits of their sport. Japanese rider Kokomo Murase does just that! She was the overall winner of the 2023-2024 World Cup season. In 2024 and 2025, she won X Games silver medals in slopestyle.

Who will the future champions be and what amazing tricks will they pull off? Fans are excited to find out!

FACT

In 2023, Murase became the first woman to land a backside triple 1440. This trick has four full rotations.

Kokomo Murase with her silver X Games medal in 2025

GLOSSARY

box (BOKS)—a low, wide feature snowboarders ride on

impress (im-PRESS)—to make someone think highly of your ability

ledge (LEJ)—a long, narrow feature snowboarders ride on

obstacle (OB-stuh-kuhl)—something that gets in the way

podium (POH-dee-uhm)—a platform where winners receive their prizes

season (SEE-zuhn)—a part of the year where certain events or activities take place

style (STILE)—the way something is done

READ MORE

Arnez, Lynda. *Be a Pro Snowboarder.* Buffalo, NY: Gareth Stevens Publishing, 2024.

Gaertner, Meg. *Snowboarding*. Mendota Heights, MN: Apex, 2022.

Krenn, Cara. *Snowboard Cross*. North Mankato, MN: Capstone, 2026.

INTERNET SITES

Kiddle: Snowboarding Facts for Kids
kids.kiddle.co/Snowboarding

Olympics: Mia Brookes
olympics.com/en/athletes/mia-brookes

X Games
xgames.com

INDEX

ABOUT THE AUTHOR

Karen Grimaldos is a writer and educator who specializes in writing for the educational market. She loves writing for kids on topics ranging from art and culture to travel and current events. Although she doesn't snowboard, she does frequently dream of living in a place with snow-covered mountains.